Life in the Desert

Written by Paul Mason

Illustrated by Andy Elkerton

What is a desert?

A desert is an area of very dry land that does not have many plants. A desert gets only a small amount of rain each year. Deserts usually lose more water than they get in rain.

Deserts are the driest places on Earth. They cover more than 20% of the Earth.

But even though deserts are tough, dry places, they are also home to many different types of life.

Hot and cold deserts

There are two main types of deserts: hot and cold.

Hot deserts have very high temperatures in the day. The highest recorded temperature for a hot desert was 56.7°C in Death Valley in California. In hot deserts, the ground is often rock, gravel or sand. There are also sand dunes – large hills of sand.

Cold deserts have much colder temperatures. Although some cold deserts have snow and ice, they are also very dry. They get almost no rain. Antarctica is a cold desert.

Famous deserts

The Sahara Desert is the world's biggest hot desert. It covers most of North Africa. It is almost the same size as the USA. Some of the sand dunes in the Sahara are 150 metres tall!

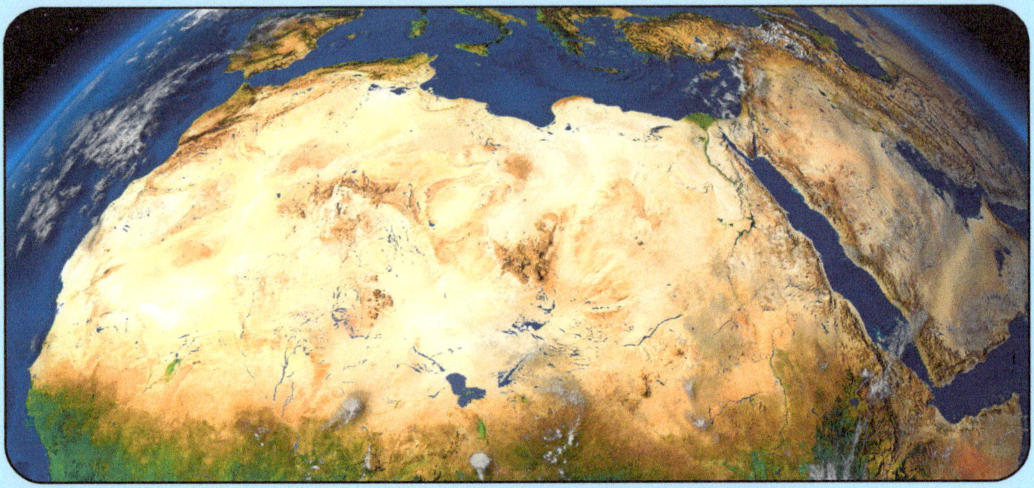

The Gobi Desert covers parts of China and Mongolia. The Gobi is a cold desert. It is the largest desert in Asia. Much of the Gobi Desert is rocky.

The Atacama Desert in Chile stretches for 1000 kilometres. The Atacama is sometimes called the 'driest place on Earth'. It has not rained in some parts of the Atacama since people first recorded the weather. Large parts of the desert are flat and covered in salt. This is because in the past there were seas where the desert is now.

But even though it is very dry, the Atacama can be quite cool. This is because a lot of the Atacama is high up.

Life in the desert

Though deserts have very little water, there are many types of animals and plants that can survive in the desert.

Perhaps the most famous desert animal is the camel. The camel is sometimes called the 'ship of the desert'. This is because a camel can travel up to 160 kilometres without drinking water! This makes camels very useful for merchants and other people travelling across the desert sands – like a ship travelling across the sea.

One of the things that helps a camel survive in the desert is its hump. The camel's hump is made of fat. A camel can use the fat when it needs water or food.

An Arabian camel, also known as a Dromedary, has one hump. A Bactrian camel has two humps.

A camel's thick coat helps protect it from the heat of the sun and the sand.

Scorpions

Scorpions also live in the desert.

Scorpions have two pincers and a long, curved tail with a stinger at the end. The scorpion's poison, or venom, is inside the stinger. A scorpion sting can be very painful. Some scorpion venom is strong enough to kill a person.

Scorpions like to make holes in the sand or ground. They mostly eat insects. If there is nothing to eat, the scorpion can slow its body down so it only needs very little food.

Gerbils

Gerbils are sometimes called 'desert rats'. They are rodents that can live in dry, hot places. They have long back feet, with large ears and eyes. They are mostly nocturnal. This means they are awake at night when it is colder.

In the Sahara, there is a type of gerbil called a 'fat-tailed' gerbil. This gerbil has a short, thick tail that stores fat and water, just like a camel's hump.

Sidewinders

The sidewinder snake lives in the deserts of North America, the Middle East and Africa.

It gets its name because of the way it moves across the sand in a sideways direction. As it moves, only two parts of the sidewinder's body touch the hot sand at the same time. This means the snake doesn't get too hot even on the hottest days.

The skin of the sidewinder is light in colour, like the desert sand. This helps the snake hide from danger.

Cactus plants

There are cactus plants in deserts all over the Americas. Cacti are many different shapes and sizes.

Cacti can survive in places with very little rain. To help save water, cacti do not have leaves like most plants. Instead, they have spines. The sharp spines help protect the cactus plant.

The thick stem of the cactus plant stores water, which animals sometimes drink. But water from a cactus can make people sick if they drink it.

People of the desert

Around the world, many people live in deserts.

The Bedouin people live in the deserts of the Middle East and North Africa. They have lived in the deserts for thousands of years. They have a long history and strong traditions.

The Bedouin keep herds of animals, like sheep, goats and camels. The Bedouin are nomadic. This means they live in tents and travel from place to place, looking for water and food for their animals. Life can be very difficult. Children do jobs to help their families.

Like the Bedouin, the Mongols of the Gobi Desert also travel across the desert, looking after animals.

The Bactrian camel is very important to the Mongols. They use camel hair to make clothes and blankets. They also drink camel milk and eat camel meat. The older children help their parents look after the animals.

Mongols live in big tents called yurts. The yurts give shade during the day and are warm at night.

Water in the desert

To survive in the desert, it is very important – and very difficult – to find water. People who travel in the desert plan their journeys carefully. They try to stop at an oasis.

An oasis is a place in the desert where there is some water, like a pond. The water comes from deep under the ground. Plants and trees can grow at an oasis. Animals and people can live at an oasis.

You can find water even in the hottest, driest desert. But sometimes, when people are very thirsty, they see an oasis when it is not really there. This is called a mirage.

The Stubborn Ship

Written by Paul Mason
Illustrated by Andy Elkerton

A long, long time ago, when the sands of the desert were still young, there was a spice merchant and his wife. Their names were Hassan and Aisha.

Hassan and Aisha sold the best spices in the whole of Al Bakra. On their stall in the market, there were bowls full of the most wonderful spices.

But though he was a good merchant, Hassan was a stubborn man.

"I don't want to listen to other people," said Hassan to his wife. "I always know best."

One morning, Hassan said to Aisha, “You look after the stall. I need to go to the camel market.”

Hassan needed to buy a camel. He wanted to take some spices across the Sahara Desert to a town far away.

“Which is the cheapest camel?” Hassan asked the camel merchant.

The merchant pointed to the most grumpy-looking camel in the market.

“That one,” he said. “The one with the big hump.”

Hassan looked at the camel. The camel looked back at Hassan.

"It looks like a strong and tough animal," said Hassan.

"Maybe you should choose a different camel," said the camel merchant. "That one is very stubborn."

"No, I want that one," said Hassan.

The next day, Hassan and Aisha carefully put their spices and their water bag onto their new camel. Then they began their journey across the desert.

The sun was strong and hot. The heat from the sand dunes was like fire. And Hassan and Aisha didn't know that their water bag leaked.

When they were a long way into the desert, Hassan noticed the empty water bag.

"What are we going to do?" said Aisha. "We can't survive in the desert without water. It's too hot and dry."

"Don't worry," said Hassan. "Look! There's an oasis."

He pulled the camel towards some trees far away. The camel didn't want to go. The camel groaned. The camel grumbled.

"Maybe the camel is right," said Aisha. "Maybe there is no oasis. Maybe it's just a mirage."

But Hassan wouldn't listen. And when they got there, there was nothing – only sand dunes.

The sun got hotter and hotter. Aisha and Hassan were very thirsty. Their mouths were dry. Even the snakes were in the shade.

Again, Hassan shouted. "Look over there! An oasis!"

He pulled the camel off the path. The camel didn't want to go. The camel groaned. The camel grumbled.

Aisha shook her head. "Husband, you should listen to the camel. It knows how to survive in the desert."

But Hassan wouldn't listen. And again, there was nothing – only rocks and gravel.

Aisha and Hassan were very hot. They were very thirsty. Their mouths were very dry. Then, Hassan saw a pond far away.

"An oasis! This time I'm sure," he shouted.

The camel didn't want to go. The camel groaned. The camel grumbled.

"When are you going to listen to the camel and stop being so stubborn?" said Aisha. "It's only a mirage."

But Hassan wouldn't listen. And once more, there was nothing – only a cactus.

Now Aisha and Hassan were very weak and tired. Their heads hurt.

Hassan saw some trees far away.

"An oasis!" he said. "We are saved! Come, camel."

He tried to pull the camel off the path.

The camel groaned. The camel grumbled. But this time, the camel wouldn't move. The camel stayed on the path. The camel didn't listen to Hassan.

"Let the camel choose the way," said Aisha. "It's only a mirage. The same as before."

"Stubborn animal," said Hassan. But Hassan was too weak to do anything.

He and Aisha closed their eyes and fell asleep.

The temperature was hotter than ever. If they didn't find water soon, it would be too late.

But the stubborn camel carried on walking, rocking from side to side, just like a ship in the sea. The camel's thick coat protected it from the sun.

Soon, there were some palm trees on the path ahead. There was a small pond and a herd of goats. There were some tents. This was the home of the nomadic Bedouin people.

But this wasn't a mirage. This was an oasis. A real oasis.

The camel groaned and walked faster.

Aisha woke up. She saw the trees. "Husband," she shouted. "We are safe!"

Hassan couldn't believe his eyes. "Is this real?"

Soon they were at the oasis. The people in the tents ran out to help them. They gave them water. The camel drank from the pond.

"That stubborn camel saved us," said Aisha. "He stayed on the path."

"That is true," said Hassan. "But remember, I was the clever person who bought him."

Activities

1 Write the answers with the words in the box.

Fat	Chile	The Sahara	A yurt	To save water
At night	The Gobi	~~Hot and cold~~		

1 What are the two main types of deserts? Hot and cold.
2 What is the world's biggest hot desert? ________________.
3 Where is the Atacama Desert? ________________.
4 What does a camel store in its hump? ________________.
5 When are gerbils awake? ________________.
6 Why do cactus plants have spines instead of leaves?

________________.

7 In which desert do the Mongols live? ________________.
8 What is a Mongol's tent called? ________________.

2 True or false? Circle the correct answer.

1	A sting from a scorpion isn't painful.	T	(F)
2	Deserts are very dry and don't get much rain.	T	F
3	Antarctica is a hot desert.	T	F
4	The camel is called the 'bicycle of the desert'.	T	F
5	The sidewinder snake gets its name because of the way it moves.	T	F
6	The Bedouin have lived in the deserts for thousands of years.	T	F
7	An oasis is a place in the desert where there is some water.	T	F

3 Number the sentences in the correct order.

a Soon, there were some palm trees on the path ahead. There was a small pond and a herd of goats. ☐

b Hassan and Aisha began their journey across the desert. ☐

c "Maybe you should choose a different camel," said the camel merchant. ☐

d One morning, Hassan said to Aisha, "You look after the stall. I need to go to the camel market." 1

e Aisha and Hassan were very hot. They were very thirsty. ☐

f The people in the tents ran out to help them. They gave them water. ☐

4 Circle the correct words.

1 The camel didn't want to go. The camel *laughed* / *cried* / *(grumbled.)*

2 On their stall in the market, there were bags full of the most wonderful *spices* / *balls* / *hats.*

3 Though he was a good merchant, Hassan was a *stubborn* / *tall* / *happy* man.

4 Hassan needed to buy a *sheep* / *horse* / *camel.*

5 The stubborn camel carried on walking, rocking from side to side, just like a ship in the *oasis* / *sea* / *pond.*

5 Write the words.

merchant ~~hump~~ camel tail foot Hassan

1 ____hump____ 2 __________ 3 __________

4 __________ 5 __________ 6 __________

6 Write the missing vowels *a*, *e*, *i*, *o* or *u*.

1 S_a_nd d_u_n_e_s are large h_i_lls of s_a_nd.

2 There are h_t and c_ld d_s_rts.

3 Many pl_nts and _n_m_ls can survive in the d_s_rt.

4 Sc_rp__ns l_k_ to m_k_ h_l_s.

5 G_rb_ls have l_ng b_ck f__t.

6 A s_d_w_nd_r is a type of sn_k_.

7 Complete the sentences with the words in the box.

~~rain~~ Dromedary driest temperature Earth

1 A desert gets only a small amount of ____rain____ each year.

2 Deserts cover more than 20% of the ____________ .

3 The highest recorded ____________ for a hot desert was 56.7°C.

4 The Atacama is sometimes called the '____________ place on Earth'.

5 An Arabian camel, also known as a ____________ , has one hump.

8 Which desert animal do you think is the most interesting? Draw and write about it.

I think the fat-tailed gerbil is the most interesting desert animal. It stores fat and water in its tail.

Bilingual Dictionary

Key: (n) = noun (v) = verb (pl) = plural (adj) = adjective (adv) = adverb

Write the words in your language.

cactus (n) ______________________
camel (n) ______________________
carefully (adv) ______________________
curved (adj) ______________________
danger (n) ______________________
desert (n) ______________________
dry (adj) ______________________
famous (adj) ______________________
fat (n) ______________________
gerbils (n pl) ______________________
gravel (n) ______________________
groaned (v) ______________________
grumbled (v) ______________________
grumpy (adj) ______________________
heat (n) ______________________
herds (n pl) ______________________
hump (n) ______________________
insects (n pl) ______________________
journeys (n pl) ______________________
leaked (v) ______________________
merchants (n pl) ______________________
mirage (n) ______________________
nocturnal (adj) ______________________
nomadic (adj) ______________________
oasis (n) ______________________
pincers (n pl) ______________________
poison (n) ______________________
pond (n) ______________________
protect (v) ______________________
rain (n) ______________________
recorded (v) ______________________
rock (n) ______________________
rocking (v) ______________________
rodents (n pl) ______________________
sand (n) ______________________
sand dunes (n pl) ______________________
scorpions (n pl) ______________________
shade (n) ______________________
ship (n) ______________________
sideways (adj) ______________________
skin (n) ______________________
snake (n) ______________________
spice (n) ______________________
spines (n pl) ______________________
stall (n) ______________________
stem (n) ______________________
sting (n) ______________________
stores (v) ______________________
stretches (v) ______________________
stubborn (adj) ______________________
survive (v) ______________________
temperature (n) ______________________
tents (n pl) ______________________
thirsty (adj) ______________________
touch (v) ______________________
tough (adj) ______________________
traditions (n pl) ______________________
venom (n) ______________________

Macmillan Education
4 Crinan Street
London N1 9XW
A division of Springer Nature Limited

Companies and representatives throughout the world

ISBN 978-1-3800-4198-2

Written by Paul Mason

First published 2014
This edition published 2019

Designed by Carolyn Gibson
Illustrated by Andy Elkerton
Picture research by Victoria Gaunt
Cover photograph by Alamy/Superstock

The author and publishers would like to thank the following for permission to reproduce their photographs: **Alamy Stock Photo**/Steve Allen Travel Photography p5, Alamy/BSIP SA p6, Alamy/Colin Harris/era-images p3(b), Alamy Stock Photo/ Arterra Picture Library pp9, 11(mr), Alamy Stock Photo/MARS/Joseph Behnken p11(br), Alamy/FLPA p12(t), Alamy/incamerastock p2, Alamy Stock Photo/PSL Images p4(t), Alamy Stock Photo/ ton koene p12 (br), Alamy Stock Photo/Nico Smit p8; **Getty Images**/benedek p1, Getty Images/Frank Wagner p4(b), Getty Images/EyeEm/Ian Chapman p7(b), Getty Images/ Corbis Unreleased p10, Getty Images/Moment/Matteo Colombo p13(bl), Getty Images/ Joshua Alan Davis p14, Getty Images/Barnabas Kindersley p13(br), Getty Images/ Mlenny Photography p7(t), Getty Images/iStock/flocu p13(t); **Photoshot**/Hemis p12(bl), Photoshot/TTL p3(t); **Springer Nature** Ltd p11(tr).

Printed and bound in Brazil

2025
10